Born in 1925

By

Kerry Butters.

Born in 1925

Millennium: 2nd millennium

Centuries: 19th century – **20th century** – 21st century

Decades: 1890s 1900s 1910s – **1920s** – 1930s 1940s
1950s

1925 (MCMXXV) was a common year starting on Thursday (dominical letter D) of the Gregorian calendar and a common year starting on Wednesday (dominical letter E) of the Julian calendar, the 1925th year of the Common Era (CE) and *Anno Domini* (AD) designations, the 925th year of the 2nd millennium, the 25th year of the 20th century, and the 6th year of the 1920s decade. Note that the Julian day for 1925 is 13 calendar days difference, which continued to be used from 1582 until the complete conversion of the Gregorian calendar was entirely done in 1929.

Contents

Events

January

- January 1 – Kristiania, the capital of Norway, reverted to its original name of Oslo.
- January 3 – Benito Mussolini made a pivotal speech in the Italian Chamber of Deputies. He took personal responsibility for the actions of his Blackshirts, challenged his political opponents to remove him from office and then promised to take charge of restoring order to Italy within forty-eight hours. Historians now trace this speech to the beginning of Mussolini's dictatorship.
- January 5 – Nellie Tayloe Ross became the first female governor (Wyoming) in the United States. Twelve days later, Ma Ferguson became first female governor of Texas.
- January 25 – Hjalmar Branting resigns as Prime Minister of Sweden because of ill health, and is replaced by the minister of trade, Rickard Sandler .

- January 27–February 1 – The 1925 serum run to Nome (the "Great Race of Mercy") relayed diphtheria antitoxin by dog sled across the U.S. territory of Alaska, to combat an epidemic.

February

- February 15 – The Alice Comedy *Alice Solves the Puzzle* was released by Disney Brothers Cartoon Studio, introducing Bootleg Pete (an early prototype for **Pegleg Pete**) for the first time.
- February 21 – *This is the cover date of the very first issue of *The New Yorker*, though not necessarily the publication date, as magazines usually date their covers ahead of time.
- February 25 – Art Gillham recorded for Columbia Records the first Western Electric masters to be commercially released.
- February 28 – The 1925 Charlevoix–Kamouraska earthquake struck northeastern North America.

March

- March 4
  - İsmet İnönü was appointed as the prime minister in Turkey (Turkey's 4th and İnönü's 3rd government).

- The inauguration of Calvin Coolidge as President of the United States was the first to be broadcast on radio.
- March 6 – *Pionerskaya Pravda*, one of the oldest children's newspapers in Europe, was founded in the Soviet Union.
- March 9–May 1 – Pink's War: The British Royal Air Force bombarded mountain strongholds of Mahsud tribesmen in South Waziristan.
- March 15 – The Phi Lambda Chi fraternity (original name "The Aztecs") was founded on the campus of Arkansas State Teacher's College in Conway, Arkansas (now the University of Central Arkansas).
- March 18 – The Tri-State Tornado, the deadliest in U.S. history, rampaged through Missouri, Illinois, and Indiana, killing 695 people and injuring 2,027. It hit the towns of Murphysboro, Illinois; Gorham, Illinois; Ellington, Missouri; and Griffin, Indiana.
- March 21 – Tennessee Governor Austin Peay signed the Butler Act, prohibiting the teaching of evolution in the state's public schools.
- March 31 – Radio station *WOWO* in Fort Wayne, Indiana began broadcasting.

April

- April–October – The *Exposition Internationale des Arts Décoratifs et Industriels Modernes* is held in Paris, giving a name to the Art Deco style.
- April 1
  - Frank Heath and his horse *Gypsy Queen* left Washington, D.C. to begin a two-year journey to visit all 48 states.
  - The Patent and Trademark Office was transferred to the Department of Commerce.
- April 10 – F. Scott Fitzgerald published *The Great Gatsby*.
- April 15 – Fritz Haarmann, a serial killer convicted of the murder of 24 boys and young men, was beheaded in Germany.
- April 16 – The Communist assault on St. Nedelya Church claims roughly 150 lives in Sofia, Bulgaria.
- April 20 – Iranian forces of Rezā Shāh occupied Ahvaz, and arrested Sheikh Khaz'al.
- April 28 – Presenting the Stanley Baldwin government's budget, Chancellor of the Exchequer Winston Churchill announced Britain's return to the gold standard.

May

- May 1 – The mausoleums in al-Baqi were destroyed by King Ibn Saud (Lanati). In the same year, he also demolishes the tombs of holy persons at Mualla Cemetery in Mecca where Muhammad's first wife Khadijah, his grandfather and other ancestors are buried. This happened despite protests by the international Islamic community.

- May 5
  - Scopes Trial: Dayton, Tennessee, biology teacher John Scopes was arrested for teaching Charles Darwin's Theory of Evolution.
  - The General Election Law was passed in Japan.
- May 8 – Tom Lee rescued 32 people from the *M.E. Norman*, a sinking steamboat.
- May 25
  - Scopes Trial: John T. Scopes was indicted for teaching Darwin's theory of evolution.
  - The National Forensic League was founded.
- May 29 – British explorer Percy Fawcett sent a last telegram to his wife, before he disappeared in the Amazon.

June

- June 1 – Percy and Florence Arrowsmith were married. This couple, who celebrated their 80th wedding anniversary June 1, 2005 (Percy aged 105, and wife Florence 100), are acknowledged by the Guinness Book of Records as record-holders for the longest marriage for a living couple and the greatest aggregate age of a married couple.

- June 6 – The Chrysler Corporation was founded by Walter Percy Chrysler.
- June 13 – Charles Francis Jenkins achieved the first synchronized transmission of pictures and sound, using 48 lines, and a mechanical system. A 10-minute film of a miniature windmill in motion was sent across 5 miles from Anacostia to Washington, D.C. The images were viewed by representatives of the National Bureau of Standards, the U.S. Navy, the Commerce Department, and others. Jenkins calls this "the first public demonstration of radiovision".
- June 14
    - The Aristotle University of Thessaloniki in Greece was founded.
    - The Turkish football club Göztepe was founded.
- June 29 – The 6.8 Mw Santa Barbara earthquake affects the central coast of California with a maximum Mercalli intensity of IX (*Violent*), destroying much of downtown Santa Barbara, California and leaving 13 people dead.

July

- July 9 – In Dublin, Ireland, Oonagh Keogh became the first female member of a stock exchange in the world.
- July 10

- ○ Scopes Trial: In Dayton, Tennessee, the so-called "Monkey Trial" began with John T. Scopes, a young high school science teacher, accused of teaching evolution in violation of a Tennessee state law.
- ○ Meher Baba begins his 44-year silence.
- July 18 – Adolf Hitler published Volume 1 of his personal manifesto *Mein Kampf*.
- July 21 – Scopes Trial: In Dayton, Tennessee, high school biology teacher John T. Scopes was found guilty of teaching evolution in class and fined $100.
- July 25 – The Telegraph Agency of the Soviet Union (TASS) was established.

August

- August 8 – The Ku Klux Klan demonstrated its popularity by holding a parade in Washington DC; as many as 40,000 male and female members of the Klan march down Pennsylvania Avenue. In 1925, an estimated 5,000,000 members belong to the Ku Klux Klan, making it the largest fraternal organization in the United States.
- August 14 – The original Hetch Hetchy Moccasin Powerhouse was completed and goes on line.
- August 25 – The French completed their evacuation of the Ruhr region of Germany.

September

- September 3 – The U.S. Navy dirigible *Shenandoah* broke up in a squall line near Caldwell, Ohio; 14 crewmen are killed.
- September 27 – Feast of the Cross according to the Old Calendar; A celestial cross appeared over Athens, Greece, while the Greek police pursues a group of Greek Old Calendarists. The phenomenon lasted for half an hour.

October

- October – The major money forgery and fraud of Alves dos Reis was exposed in Portugal.
- October 1 – Mount Rushmore National Memorial was dedicated in South Dakota.

Locarno Treaties with Gustav Stresemann, Austen Chamberlain and Aristide Briand

- October 2 – In London
  - John Logie Baird successfully transmitted the first television pictures with a greyscale image.
  - The city's first enclosed double-decker buses were introduced.

- October 5–16 – The Locarno Treaties were negotiated.
- October 8 – Cubana de Aviación was founded.

November

- November 5 – Secret agent Sidney Reilly is executed by the OGPU, the secret police of the Soviet Union.
- November 14 – The first Surrealist art exhibition opened in Paris.
- November 24 – The silent film *El Húsar de la Muerte* was released in Santiago, Chile.
- November 26 – Prajadhipok (Rama VII) was crowned as King of Siam.
- November 28 – The weekly country music-variety radio program *Grand Ole Opry* was first broadcast on WSM radio in Nashville, Tennessee, as the "WSM Barn Dance".

December

- December 1 – The Locarno Treaties were signed in London.
- December 11 – Pope Pius XI's encyclical *Quas primas*, on the Feast of Christ the King, is promulgated.

Reza Shah

- December 16
  - Reza Shah became shah of Persia.
  - Alpha Phi Omega, a National service fraternity, was founded at Lafayette College.
  - Colombo Radio launched in Ceylon; the station was subsequently known as *Radio Ceylon*.
- December 25 – IG Farben was formed by the merger of six chemical companies in Germany.

Paris Rue de Montmartre in 1925

Date unknown

- Spring – Leica I 35 mm film still camera introduced.
- The Australian state of Queensland introduced a 44-hour working week.
- The Brisbane City Council, (Brisbane, Australia), was created from the amalgamation of 20 smaller cities, towns and shires.

- New York City became the largest city in the world, taking the lead from London.
- The Thompson submachine gun sold for $175 in the 1925 Sears, Roebuck and Company mail order catalog.
- The National Football League added 5 teams: the New York Giants, Detroit Panthers, Providence Steam Roller, a new Canton Bulldogs team, and the Pottsville Maroons.
- In Germany, the Bauhaus moved to a building in Dessau designed by Walter Gropius.
- Lion Feuchtwanger's novel *Jud Süß* published.
- The Shueisha Publishing Company was founded in Tokyo.
- The Wheel gymnastics was invented in Germany.

Births

January

Paul Newman

Douglas Engelbart

- January 1 – Paul Bomani, Tanzanian politician and ambassador (d. 2005)
- January 2
  - Larry Harmon, American entertainer and TV producer (*Bozo the Clown*) (d. 2008)
  - Eraño de Guzman Manalo, 2nd Executive Minister (*Tagapamahalang Pangkalahatan*) of the *Iglesia ni Cristo* (Church of Christ) (d. 2009)
- January 4 – Veikko Hakulinen, Finnish cross-country skier (d. 2003)
- January 6 – John DeLorean, American car maker (d. 2005)
- January 7 – Gerald Durrell, British naturalist, zookeeper, author, and television presenter (d. 1995)
- January 8 – Helmuth Hübener, German youth political activist against the Hitler regime (d. 1942)
- January 9 – Lee Van Cleef, American actor (d. 1989)
- January 11 – Grant Tinker, American television executive
- January 13

- ○ Georgi Kaloyanchev, Bulgarian actor (d. 2012)
- ○ Gwen Verdon, American actress and dancer (d. 2000)
- January 14 – Yukio Mishima, Japanese writer (d. 1970)
- January 17 – Duane Hanson, American sculptor (d. 1996)
- January 21 – Charles Aidman, American actor (d. 1993)
- January 25 – Gilles Deleuze, French philosopher (d. 1995)
- January 26
  - ○ Joan Leslie, American actress (d. 2015)
  - ○ Paul Newman, American actor, entrepreneur and philanthropist (d. 2008)
- January 29 – Robert W. McCollum, American epidemiologist, (d. 2010)
- January 30
  - ○ Douglas Engelbart, American inventor (d. 2013)
  - ○ Dorothy Malone, American actress

February

Jack Lemmon

George Kennedy

- February 1 – Mary Nesbitt, American female professional baseball player (d. 2013)
- February 2 – Elaine Stritch, American actress (d. 2014)
- February 3
  - Leon Schlumpf, Swiss Federal Councillor (d. 2012)
  - John Fiedler, American actor (d. 2005)
- February 7 – Hans Schmidt, Canadian professional wrestler (d. 2012)
- February 8 – Jack Lemmon, American actor and film director (*The Odd Couple*) (d. 2001)
- February 10 – Pierre Mondy, French film and theatre actor and director (d. 2012)
- February 11
  - Kim Stanley, American actress (d. 2001)
  - Virginia E. Johnson, American sexologist (d. 2013)
- February 17
  - Ron Goodwin, English composer and conductor (d. 2003)

- o Hal Holbrook, American actor (*Mark Twain Tonight*)
- February 18 – George Kennedy, American actor (*Cool Hand Luke*) (d. 2016)
- February 20
  - o Robert Altman, American film director (d. 2006)
  - o Pat Lanigan, Australian public servant (d. 1992)
- February 21 – Sam Peckinpah, American director (d. 1984)
- February 25
  - o Maddy English, American female baseball player (d. 2004)
  - o Shehu Shagari, President of Nigeria from 1979 to 1983
- February 26 – Everton Weekes, West Indian cricketer
- February 27 – Samuel Dash, American Watergate Congressional counsel (d. 2004)

March

- March 4 – Paul Mauriat, French musician (*Love is Blue*) (d. 2006)
- March 7 – Rene Gagnon, U.S. Marine flag raiser on Iwo Jima (d. 1979)
- March 12 – Leo Esaki, Japanese physicist, Nobel Prize laureate
- March 16
  - o Cornell Borchers, German actress (d. 2014)

- ○ Luis E. Miramontes, Mexican chemist (d. 2004)
- March 17 – Gabriele Ferzetti, Italian actor (d. 2015)
- March 22 – Gerard Hoffnung, German-born English humorist (d. 1959)
- March 23 – David Watkin, British cinematographer (d. 2008)
- March 25 – Flannery O'Connor, American writer (d. 1964)
- March 26 – Pierre Boulez, French composer (d. 2016)
- March 29 – Bobby Hutchins, Our Gang child star (d. 1945)

April

Hans Rosenthal

Rod Steiger

- April – Qassem Al-Nasser, Jordanian General (d. 2007)

- April 2 – Hans Rosenthal, German radio editor, director, and one of the most popular German radio and television hosts of the 1970s and 80s (d. 1987)
- April 3 – Tony Benn, British politician (d. 2014)
- April 4 – Fariza Magomadova, Chechen educator and boarding school director
- April 7 – Chaturanan Mishra, Indian politician (d. 2011)
- April 14
  - Gene Ammons, American jazz saxophonist (d. 1974)
  - Rod Steiger, American actor (*In The Heat Of The Night*) (d. 2002)
- April 18 – Bob Hastings, American actor (d. 2014)
- April 19 – Hugh O'Brian, American actor
- April 20
  - Elena Verdugo, American actress
  - Ernie Stautner, German-born American football player (d. 2006)
- April 21- Solomon Perel, Israeli motivational speaker
- April 22 – George Cole, English actor (d. 2015)
- April 24
  - Faye Dancer, American baseball player (d. 2002)
  - Eugen Weber, Romanian-born historian (d. 2007)
- April 25 – Kay E. Kuter, American actor (d. 2003)
- April 26
  - Jørgen Ingmann, Danish musician (d. 2015)
  - Michele Ferrero, Italian businessman (d. 2015)

May

Pol Pot

Malcolm X

Jeanne Crain

- May 1
    - Scott Carpenter, American astronaut (d. 2013)
    - Anna May Hutchison, American professional baseball player (d. 1998)
- May 2

- Inga Gill, Swedish actress (d. 2000)
- John Neville, English actor (d. 2011)
- Maria Barroso, Portuguese politician and actress (d. 2015)
- Lou Rowan, Australian Test cricket match umpire
- May 3 – Jean Séguy, French sociologist of religions (d. 2007)
- May 4
  - Maurice R. Greenberg, American businessman
  - Olive Osmond, Osmond family matriarch (d. 2004)
  - Jenő Buzánszky, Hungarian footballer (d. 2015)
- May 5 – Charles Chaplin Jr., American actor (d. 1968)
- May 8 – Ali Hassan Mwinyi, Tanzanian president
- May 12 – Yogi Berra, American baseball player (d. 2015)
- May 14
  - Sophie Kurys, American professional baseball player (d. 2013)
  - Patrice Munsel, American opera singer
- May 15 – Andrei Eshpai, Russian pianist (d. 2015)
- May 19
  - Pol Pot, Cambodian Khmer Rouge leader (d. 1998)
  - Malcolm X, African-American civil rights activist (d. 1965)
  -

- May 22
  - James King, American tenor (d. 2005)
  - Jean Tinguely, Swiss painter and sculptor (d. 1991)
- May 23 – Joshua Lederberg, American molecular biologist, recipient of the Nobel Prize in Physiology or Medicine (d. 2008)
- May 24 – Mai Zetterling, Swedish actress and film director (d. 1994)
- May 25
  - Jeanne Crain, American actress (d. 2003)
  - José María Gatica, Argentine boxer (d. 1963)
- May 26 – Alec McCowen, English actor
- May 28
  - Dietrich Fischer-Dieskau, German lyric baritone and conductor (d. 2012)
  - Pavel Štěpán, Czech pianist (d. 1998)
- May 31 – Frei Otto, German architect (d. 2015)

June

Tony Curtis

Barbara Bush

Giorgio Napolitano

- June 1 – Dilia Díaz Cisneros, Venezuelan teacher
- June 3 – Tony Curtis, American actor (d. 2010)
- June 7 – John Biddle, American yachting cinematographer and lecturer (d. 2008)
- June 8 – Barbara Bush, First Lady of the United States
- June 11 – William Styron, American writer (d. 2006)
- June 14 – Pierre Salinger, White House Press Secretary (d. 2004)
- June 20 – Audie Murphy, American World War II hero and actor (d. 1971)
- June 21 – Maureen Stapleton, American actress (d. 2006)
- June 25
    - Robert Venturi, American architect

- ○ June Lockhart, American actress
- June 26 – Richard X. Slattery, American actor (d. 1997)
- June 29
  - ○ Giorgio Napolitano, Italian politician
  - ○ Cara Williams, American actress

July

- July 1 – Farley Granger, American actor (d. 2011)
- July 2
  - ○ Medgar Evers, African-American civil rights activist (d. 1963)
  - ○ Patrice Lumumba, Congolese independence leader (d. 1961)
- July 6
  - ○ Merv Griffin, American game show developer and host (d. 2007)
  - ○ Bill Haley, American musician (*Bill Haley & His Comets*) (d. 1981)
- July 10 – Mahathir bin Mohamad, fourth Prime Minister of Malaysia
- July 11 – David Graham, British actor and voice artist.
- July 12
  - ○ Roger Bonham Smith, former chairman and CEO of General Motors (d. 2007)
  - ○ Rosie Harris, English author
- July 14 – Hugh Gillin, American actor (d. 2004)
- July 20

- o Frantz Fanon, French-Algerian psychiatrist and philosopher (d. 1961)
  - o Jacques Delors, French politician
- July 22 – Joseph Sargent, American film director (d. 2014)
- July 23 – Gloria DeHaven, American actress
- July 26 – Ana María Matute, Spanish writer (d. 2014)
- July 28 – Baruch S. Blumberg, American scientist, recipient of the Nobel Prize in Physiology or Medicine (d. 2011)
- July 29
  - o Shivram Dattatreya Phadnis, Indian cartoonist
  - o Mikis Theodorakis, Greek composer
- July 30 – Alexander Trocchi, Scottish writer (d. 1984)
- July 31 – Carmel Quinn, Irish-American singer and performer

August

Jorge Rafael Videla

Alija Izetbegović

Oscar Peterson

Donald O'Connor

- August 2
  - Jorge Rafael Videla, 42nd President of Argentina (d. 2013)
  - Alan Whicker, British television presenter (d. 2013)
- August 3 – Dom Um Romão, Brazilian jazz drummer (d. 2005)
- August 4 – Betty Trezza, Italian-American female professional baseball player (d. 2007)

- August 7 – M. S. Swaminathan, Indian scientist
- August 8 – Alija Izetbegović, President of Bosnia-Herzegovina (d. 2003)
- August 9 – David A. Huffman, American computer scientist (d. 1999)
- August 11
  - Arlene Dahl, American actress
  - Mike Douglas, American entertainer (d. 2006)
- August 12
  - Norris McWhirter (d. 2004) and his twin brother,
  - Ross McWhirter (d. 1975), Scottish co-founders of the *Guinness Book of Records*
- August 15
  - Mike Connors, American actor
  - Ruth Lessing, American female professional baseball player (d. 2000)
  - Oscar Peterson, Canadian jazz pianist (d. 2007)
  - Bill Pinkney, American performer and singer (d. 2007)
  - Aldo Ciccolini, Italian-born French pianist (d. 2015)
- August 16 – Kirke Mechem, American composer
- August 22
  - Honor Blackman, English actress
  - Terry Donahue, Canadian female professional baseball player
- August 25 – Thea Astley, Australian writer (d. 2004)

- August 26 – Jack Hirshleifer, American economist (d. 2005)
- August 27 – Nat Lofthouse, English footballer (d. 2011)
- August 28
  - Donald O'Connor, American actor, singer, and dancer (d. 2003)
  - José Parra Martínez, Spanish footballer (d. 2016)
- August 29 – Demetrio Basilio Lakas Bahas, former President of Panama (d. 1999)
- August 30 – Laurent de Brunhoff, French writer and illustrator
- August 31
  - Maurice Pialat, French actor and director (d. 2003)
  - Pete Vonachen, American restaurateur and baseball team owner (d. 2013)

September

Peter Sellers

B. B. King

- September 3 – Shoista Mullojonova, Tajik-born Shashmakom singer (d. 2010)
- September 7 – Laura Ashley, Welsh designer (d. 1985)
- September 8 – Peter Sellers, English comedian and actor (*The Pink Panther*) (d. 1980)
- September 10 – Boris Alexandrovich Tchaikovsky, Russian composer (d. 1996)
- September 13 – Mel Tormé, American musician (d. 1999)
- September 15 – Helle Virkner, Danish actress (d. 2009)
- September 16
  - Charles Haughey, sixth Taoiseach (head of government of the Republic of Ireland) (d. 2006)
  - B.B. King, American singer-songwriter and guitarist (d. 2015)
- September 19 – Franklin Sousley, U.S. Marine flag raiser on Iwo Jima (d. 1945)
- September 23 – Denis Twitchett, Cambridge scholar and Chinese historian (d. 2006)
- September 24 – Autar Singh Paintal, Indian medical scientist (d. 2004)
- September 25

- ○ Paul B. MacCready, Jr., American aeronautical engineer (d. 2007)
  - ○ Silvana Pampanini, Italian actress (d. 2016)
- September 27 – Robert G. Edwards, British Nobel physiologist (d. 2013)
- September 28
  - ○ Cromwell Everson, South African composer (d. 1991)
  - ○ Carolyn Morris, American female professional baseball player (d. 1996)
- September 30 – Arkady Ostashev, Soviet engineer and rocket scientist (d. 1998)

October

Margaret Thatcher

Angela Lansbury

Johnny Carson

- October 1
  - Christine Pullein-Thompson, British author (d. 2005)
  - Diana Pullein-Thompson, British author (d. 2015)
- October 3 – Gore Vidal, American author (d. 2012)
- October 5 – Gail Davis, American actress (d. 1997)
- October 7 – Mildred Earp, American female professional baseball player
- October 11 – Elmore Leonard, American novelist (d. 2013)
- October 13
  - Lenny Bruce, American comic (d. 1966)
  - Margaret Thatcher, Prime Minister of the United Kingdom from 1979 to 1990 (d. 2013)
- October 16 – Angela Lansbury, English-born U.S. actress
- October 20
  - Art Buchwald, American humorist and columnist (d. 2007)

- ○ Gene Wood, American game show announcer (d. 2004)
- October 21 – Celia Cruz, Cuban-American singer (d. 2003)
- October 22 – Robert Rauschenberg, American painter and graphic artist (d. 2008)
- October 23 – Johnny Carson, American comedian and television host (*The Tonight Show*) (d. 2005)
- October 24
  - ○ Bob Azzam, Egyptian singer (d. 2004)
  - ○ Luciano Berio, Italian composer (d. 2003)
  - ○ Al Feldstein, American artist and comic book creator (d. 2014)
- October 27 – Warren Christopher, American diplomat (d. 2011)
- October 29
  - ○ Dominick Dunne, American writer (d. 2009)
  - ○ Robert Hardy, English actor
  - ○ Klaus Roth, British mathematician (d. 2015)
- October 31 – John Pople, English chemist, Nobel Prize laureate (d. 2004)

November

Richard Burton

Rock Hudson

Robert Kennedy

- November 4 – Doris Roberts, American actress (d. 2016)
- November 9 – Giovanni Coppa, Italian cardinal (d. 2016)
- November 10 – Richard Burton, Welsh actor (*Cleopatra*) (d. 1984)
- November 11
  - Jonathan Winters, American actor and comedian (d. 2013)
  - John Guillermin, British director (d. 2015)
- November 12 – Heinz Schubert, German actor (d. 1999)
- November 17 – Rock Hudson, American actor (d. 1985)
- November 18 – Gene Mauch, baseball manager (d. 2005)

- November 20
  - Kaye Ballard, American comedian (*The Mothers-in-Law*)
  - Robert F. Kennedy, American politician and Attorney General of the United States (d. 1968)
  - Mark Miller, American actor
  - Maya Plisetskaya, Russian ballerina (d. 2015)
- November 22 – Gunther Schuller, American musician (d. 2015)
- November 23 – Maria di Gerlando, American operatic soprano (d. 2010)
- November 24
  - William F. Buckley, Jr., American journalist, author, and commentator (*The Firing Line*) (d. 2008)
  - Simon van der Meer, Dutch physicist, Nobel Prize laureate (d. 2011)
- November 26 – Eugene Istomin, American pianist (d. 2003)
- November 27
  - John Maddox, Welsh science writer (d. 2009)
  - Ernie Wise, English comedian (d. 1999)
- November 30 – William H. Gates, Sr., American attorney, father of Bill Gates

December

Julie Harris

Sammy Davis, Jr.

Dick Van Dyke

- December 1 – Martin Rodbell, American scientist, recipient of the Nobel Prize in Physiology or Medicine (d. 1998)
- December 2 – Julie Harris, American actress (d. 2013)
- December 3 – Erik Mørk, Danish actor (d. 1993)

- December 4 – Lino Lacedelli, Italian mountaineer (d. 2009)
- December 8 – Sammy Davis Jr., American singer, dancer, musician, and actor (d. 1990)
- December 11 – Paul Greengard, American neuroscientist, recipient of the Nobel Prize in Physiology or Medicine
- December 12 – Vladimir Shainsky, Soviet and Russian composer
- December 13 – Dick Van Dyke, American actor, singer, dancer and comedian (*The Dick Van Dyke Show*)
- December 15
  - Hiroshi Motoyama, Japanese scientist
  - Kasey Rogers, American actress (d. 2006)
- December 19
  - Rabah Bitat, former President of Algeria (d. 2000)
  - Robert B. Sherman, American songwriter (d. 2012)
- December 21 – Dorothy Kamenshek, American professional baseball player (d. 2010)
- December 23 – Duncan Hallas, prominent member of the Trotskyist movement in Great Britain (d. 2002)
- December 25 – Dorothy Mueller, American professional baseball player (d. 1985)
- December 28
  - Hildegard Knef, German actress, singer and writer (d. 2002)

- Milton Obote, President of Uganda (d. 2005)
- December 29 – Pete Dye, American golf course architect

Date unknown

- Godrej Sidhwa, Pakistani theologist (d. 2011)

Deaths

January

- January 4 – Nellie Cashman, Irish-born prospector (b. 1845)
- January 8 – George Bellows, American artist (b. 1882)
- January 14
  - Camille Decoppet, Swiss Federal Councilor (b. 1852)
  - Harry Furniss, English cartoonist, illustrator and pioneer animator (b. 1854)
- January 16 – Aleksey Kuropatkin, Russian general and Imperial Russian Minister of War (b. 1848)
- January 18 – Charles Lanrezac, French general (b. 1852)
- January 22 – Fanny Bullock Workman, American geographer, writer and mountain climber (b. 1859)
- January 25
  - Alexander Kaulbars, Russian general and explorer (b. 1844)

- January 26
  - Caspar F. Goodrich, American admiral (b. 1847)
  - Sir James Mackenzie, Scottish cardiologist (b. 1853)
- January 31 – George Washington Cable, American writer (b. 1844)

February

Friedrich Ebert

- February 2 – Jaap Eden, Dutch speed skater (b. 1873)
- February 3 – Oliver Heaviside, English mathematician (b. 1850)
- February 4 – Robert Koldewey, German architect and archaeologist (b. 1855)
- February 10 – Aristide Bruant, French singer and nightclub owner (b. 1851)
- February 11 – H. E. Beunke, Dutch writer (b. 1851)
- February 18 – James Lane Allen, American writer (b. 1849)
- February 24 – Hjalmar Branting, Prime Minister of Sweden, recipient of the Nobel Peace Prize (b. 1860)

- February 25 – Louis Feuillade, French silent film director (b. 1873)
- February 28 – Friedrich Ebert, President of Germany (Weimar Republic) (b. 1871)

March

Lucille Ricksen

- March 2 – Luigj Gurakuqi, Albanian writer and politician (assassinated) (b. 1879)
- March 4
  - Moritz Moszkowski, Polish composer (b. 1854)
  - James Ward, English philosopher and psychologist (b. 1843)
  - John Montgomery Ward, American baseball player and MLB Hall of Famer (b. 1860)
- March 7 – Georgy Evgenyevich Lvov, Prime Minister of Russia (b. 1861)
- March 8 – Juliette Wytsman, Belgian painter (b. 1866)
- March 10 – Myer Prinstein, American track athlete (b. 1878)
- March 12

- o Gergely Luthár, Hungarian Slovene writer (b. 1841)
- o Sun Yat-sen, Chinese revolutionary (b. 1866)
- March 13 – Lucille Ricksen, American silent film actress (b. 1910)
- March 14 – Walter Camp, American football coach (b. 1859)
- March 20 – George Curzon, 1st Marquess Curzon of Kedleston, Viceroy of India (b. 1859)
- March 28 – Henry Rawlinson, 1st Baron Rawlinson, British general (b. 1864)
- March 30 – Rudolf Steiner, Austrian philosopher (b. 1861)

April

- April 6 – Alexandra Kitchin, British model for Lewis Carroll (b. 1864)
- April 7 – Patriarch Tikhon of Moscow, Patriarch of the Russian Orthodox Church (b. 1865)
- April 13 – Elwood Haynes, American inventor (b. 1857)
- April 14 – John Singer Sargent, American artist (b. 1856)
- April 15
  - o Fritz Haarmann, German serial killer (executed) (b. 1879)

Fritz Haarmann

-
  - August Endell, German architect (b. 1871)
- April 19 – John Walter Smith, American politician (b. 1845)
- April 22 – André Caplet, French composer and conductor (b. 1878)

May

- May 2
  - Johann Palisa, Austrian astronomer (b. 1848)
  - Antun Branko Šimić, Croatian poet (b. 1898)
- May 3 – Clement Ader, French Army Captain and aviation pioneer (b. 1841)
- May 7
  - William Hesketh Lever, English industrialist, Philanthropist and politician (b. 1851)
  - Doveton Sturdee, British admiral (b. 1859)
- May 10 – William Massey, Prime Minister of New Zealand (b.1856)
- May 12
  - Amy Lowell, American poet (b. 1874)

- ○ Charles Mangin, French general (b. 1866)
- May 14 – H. Rider Haggard, English writer (b. 1856)
- May 15 – Nelson A. Miles, American general (b. 1839)
- May 20
  - ○ Elias M. Ammons, Governor of Colorado (b. 1860)
  - ○ Joseph Howard, 1st Prime Minister of Malta (b. 1862)
- May 21 – Hidesaburō Ueno, Japanese agricultural scientist and guardian of Hachikō (b. 1871)
- May 22 – John French, 1st Earl of Ypres, British World War I field marshal (b. 1852)
- May 31 – John Palm, Curaçao born composer (b. 1885)

June

Lucien Guitry

- June 1
  - ○ Lucien Guitry, French actor (b. 1860)
  - ○ Thomas R. Marshall, Vice President of the United States (b. 1854)
- June 2 – James Ellsworth, American mine owner and banker (b. 1849)

- June 3 – Camille Flammarion, French astronomer (b. 1842)
- June 16 – Emmett Hardy, American jazz cornetist (b. 1903)
- June 17 – Adolf Pilar von Pilchau, Baltic German politician, regent of the United Baltic Duchy and baron (b. 1851)
- June 18 – Robert M. La Follette Sr., American politician (b. 1855)
- June 20 – Josef Breuer, Austrian neurologist (b. 1842)
- June 22 – Felix Klein, German mathematician (b. 1849)
- June 29 – Christian Michelsen, first Prime Minister of Norway (b. 1857)

July

- July 1 – Erik Satie, French composer (b. 1866)
- July 2 – Nikolai Golitsyn last Prime Minister of the Russian Empire (executed) (b. 1850)
- July 7 – Clarence Hudson White American photographer (b. 1871)
- July 14 – Pancho Villa, Filipino world boxing champion (b. 1901)
- July 17 – Lovis Corinth, German painter (b. 1858)
- July 26
    - Antonio Ascari, Italian race car driver (b. 1888)
    - William Jennings Bryan, American lawyer and politician (b. 1860) (diabetes and fatigue)

- ○ Gottlob Frege, German mathematician and philosopher (b. 1848)
- July 30 – William Wynn Westcott, British Freemason (b. 1848)

August

- August 6 – Gregorio Ricci-Curbastro, Italian mathematician (b. 1853)
- August 12 – Severo Fernández, former President of Bolivia (b. 1849)
- August 15 – Konrad Mägi, Estonian landscape painter (b. 1878)
- August 17 – Ioan Slavici, Romanian writer (b. 1848)
- August 25 – Franz Conrad von Hötzendorf, Austrian field marshal (b. 1852)

September

- September 7 – René Viviani, Prime Minister of France (b. 1863)
- September 16 – Alexander Alexandrovich Friedman, Russian mathematician (b. 1888)
- September 17 – Carl Eytel, German-American artist working in Palm Springs, California (b. 1862)
- September 29 – Léon Bourgeois, French statesman, recipient of the Nobel Peace Prize (b. 1851)

October

- October 7 – Christy Mathewson, American baseball player and MLB Hall of Famer (b. 1880)
- October 14 – Eugen Sandow, German-born bodybuilder, physical culturist (b. 1867)
- October 31
  - Mikhail Frunze, Russian Bolshevik leader (b. 1885)
  - Max Linder, French silent film actor (b. 1883) (suicide)

November

- November 1 – Lester Cuneo, American actor (b. 1888)
- November 3 – Lucile McVey, American actress, part of comedy team with her late husband Sidney Drew (b. 1890)
- November 6 – Khải Định, Emperor of Vietnam (b. 1885)
- November 20
  - Queen Alexandra, consort of Edward VII of the United Kingdom (b. 1844)
  - Clara Morris, Victorian stage actress (b. 1846)
- November 21 – Robert Wrenn, American tennis player (b. 1873)
- November 25 – King Vajiravudh of Siam (b. 1880)

December

Władysław Reymont

- December 5 – Władysław Reymont, Polish writer, Nobel Prize laureate (b. 1867)
- December 8 – Marguerite Marsh, American actress (b. 1888)
- December 9 – Pablo Iglesias, co-founder of the Spanish Socialist Workers Party (b. 1850)
- December 13 – Antonio Maura, Spanish conservative politician, former Prime Minister (b. 1853)
- December 15 – Battling Siki, Senegalese boxer (b. 1897)
- December 19 – José Ignacio Quintón, Puerto Rican composer and pianist (b. 1881)
- December 21
    - Lottie Lyell, Australian female pioneer film director and producer (b. 1890)
    - Jules Méline, Prime Minister of France (b. 1838)
- December 22
    - Alice, Princess Dowager of Monaco, consort of Albert I of Monaco (b. 1858)

- Mary Thurman, American actress (b. 1895)
- December 25 – Karl Abraham, German psychoanalyst (b. 1877)
- December 28
  - Raymond P. Rodgers, American admiral (b. 1849)
  - Sergei Aleksandrovich Yesenin, Russian lyrical poet (b. 1895)
- December 29 – Félix Vallotton, Swiss painter (b. 1865)
- December 31 – J. Gordon Edwards, Canadian film director (b. 1867)

Nobel Prizes

- Physics – James Franck and Gustav Ludwig Hertz
- Chemistry – Richard Adolf Zsigmondy
- Physiology or Medicine – not awarded
- Literature – George Bernard Shaw
- Peace – Austen Chamberlain and Charles Gates Dawes

In the News

The First Motel (Motorists Hotel) opens in San Luis Obispo, California.

A giant tornado struck Missouri, Illinois and Indiana.

The Grand Ole Opry begins broadcasting.

More and more Airlines are formed around the world for Freight mail and passenger traffic.

The Scopes Monkey Trial comes to an end.

Field Marshall Hindenburg is elected president of Germany .

The Mount Rushmore National Monument site was dedicated during October.

A major epidemic of Diphtheria breaks out on February 2nd in Alaska.

1925 Calendar

January 1925

Sun	Mon	Tue	Wed	Thu	Fri	Sat
				1	2	3
4	5	6	7	8	9	10
11	12	13	14	15	16	17
18	19	20	21	22	23	24
25	26	27	28	29	30	31

February 1925

Sun	Mon	Tue	Wed	Thu	Fri	Sat
1	2	3	4	5	6	7
8	9	10	11	12	13	14
15	16	17	18	19	20	21
22	23	24	25	26	27	28

March 1925

Sun	Mon	Tue	Wed	Thu	Fri	Sat
1	2	3	4	5	6	7
8	9	10	11	12	13	14
15	16	17	18	19	20	21
22	23	24	25	26	27	28
29	30	31				

April 1925

Sun	Mon	Tue	Wed	Thu	Fri	Sat
		1	2	3	4	
5	6	7	8	9	10	11
12	13	14	15	16	17	18
19	20	21	22	23	24	25
26	27	28	29	30		

May 1925

Sun	Mon	Tue	Wed	Thu	Fri	Sat
					1	2
3	4	5	6	7	8	9
10	11	12	13	14	15	16
17	18	19	20	21	22	23
24	25	26	27	28	29	30
31						

June 1925

Sun	Mon	Tue	Wed	Thu	Fri	Sat
	1	2	3	4	5	6
7	8	9	10	11	12	13
14	15	16	17	18	19	20
21	22	23	24	25	26	27
28	29	30				

July 1925

Sun	Mon	Tue	Wed	Thu	Fri	Sat
			1	2	3	4
5	6	7	8	9	10	11
12	13	14	15	16	17	18
19	20	21	22	23	24	25
26	27	28	29	30	31	

August 1925

Sun	Mon	Tue	Wed	Thu	Fri	Sat
						1
2	3	4	5	6	7	8
9	10	11	12	13	14	15
16	17	18	19	20	21	22
23	24	25	26	27	28	29
30	31					

September 1925

Sun	Mon	Tue	Wed	Thu	Fri	Sat
		1	2	3	4	5
6	7	8	9	10	11	12
13	14	15	16	17	18	19
20	21	22	23	24	25	26
27	28	29	30			

October 1925

Sun	Mon	Tue	Wed	Thu	Fri	Sat
				1	2	3
4	5	6	7	8	9	10
11	12	13	14	15	16	17
18	19	20	21	22	23	24
25	26	27	28	29	30	31

November 1925

Sun	Mon	Tue	Wed	Thu	Fri	Sat
1	2	3	4	5	6	7
8	9	10	11	12	13	14
15	16	17	18	19	20	21
22	23	24	25	26	27	28
29	30					

December 1925

Sun	Mon	Tue	Wed	Thu	Fri	Sat
		1	2	3	4	5
6	7	8	9	10	11	12
13	14	15	16	17	18	19
20	21	22	23	24	25	26
27	28	29	30	31		

19513015R00031

Printed in Great Britain
by Amazon